THE CALL TO THE PLAGUED MINDS

Caylene Judaea Augustin

BookLeaf Publishing

India | USA | UK

The Call To The Plagued Minds

© 2021 Caylene Judaea Augustin

All rights reserved.

No part of this publication may be reproduced, stored in a retrieval system, or transmitted, in any form or by any means, electronic, mechanical, photocopying, recording or otherwise, without the prior written permission of the presenters.

Caylene Judaea Augustin asserts the moral right to be identified as author of this work.

Presentation by *BookLeaf Publishing*

Web: www.bookleafpub.com

E-mail: info@bookleafpub.com

ISBN: 9789358739152

First edition 2021

DEAR PERSON READING THIS

If you picked this up, then I believe something called you to
this text. I hope you are encouraged, or at least heard in the
following words.

P.S

I've been there too

Thanks Cyrenity, for making me take this opportunity,

and thanks Mom, for not letting me quit. In anything.

Ever.

1. THE GIRL WITH THE WORLD ON HER SHOULDERS

To the Girl with the World on her Shoulders, And
mountains left to climb.
You hold your own and you overcome,
Seeming unweathered by time

To the Girl with the World on her shoulders, And
who treks through the strongest storms. You survive
and you walk on,
Even with your soul torn

To the Girl with the World on her Shoulders, Who
sees those who struggle to stand. You go back and
help carry their mountain, Till they find their feet
again

But the Girl with the World on her Shoulders Bears
more by the passing day,
And she may even need to ask for help, But
may be too afraid to say

To the Girl With the World on her Shoulders, From a
Friend who has able hands, I'll help carry your
mountains too

I want to help you stand.

My mountains may look big and scary, And from my
perspective yours do too. But I still want to be able to

lighten your load And help you smile through.

So never be afraid to ask,
As I will never ever say no.
No matter what our problems are,
I know I won't let go.

2. FAKE IT TILL YOU MAKE IT

Fake it till you make it
Such a common and powerful phrase But faking
it can become too easy when You don't know
the rest of the way

The days grow long and weary To the point
where they feel like years When will I see the
finish line?? Many ask with pleas and tears

Making it seems too far away
So encouragement falls on deaf ears The pain
has melded to become one With the person
you've held most dear

So when that smile once in a while
Comes to grace their face
Remember they have more fear and pain As they
fake it to run the race

3. SOUL

When something weighs down on our soul It feels
different than a physical weight Like someone put a
whole in your being Or someone left open our
emotional gate

The happy times and the sad ones
The rage and the grief
It all loses their glamour and tone
As the memories fall into its sea

When our soul is hurting
Our seas become woeful,
Stripping memories of their color and tone So every joy
and memory of bright yellow Fall grey as they recalled to
mind, making us feel alone

For those who do not see the waves under every laugh,
cackle and grin
They can't possibly understand the gaping whole within

4. THE PATH

I know the path from whence I came.
I came from the love of two people once separated by
oceans.
From the places where breezes swayed the trees From a
heart that bore music and moved in dance From a poet with
a god given gift

I know the path from whence I started From my mother
walking down the aisle Joining hands with a man God gave
her to have One that was wonderfully on the other side of
her spectrum
Beginning the string of events that can only be called
miracles

I know the path from which my enemies hunt The
path from whence demons run
From whence my darkest thoughts take form And
haunt from parts hidden from sun

I know the path from whence help comes Though
even then the demons tear apart The perverted ropes
that burn at the touch As my thoughts turn into
weapons that hurt

13

I know the path to where I go
When I'm called or this path is done
Where release may find me and my mind is calm Where my
body rests in its final home

But till then I walk my path alone

Hoping and praying for sight

For my might is lacked and I flew from help From fear and pain, and I won't go back

Is this stubbornness and pride

Or is it another perverted reason?

I'd rather not try to find out

In my confusion a hand still prods me forward, with two footsteps before me

So I shall silently walk the path guiding me home 14

5. EDUCATION

Students ask this question
In academic frustration and strife
"Why do I have to learn this?
I won't use it in life."

But here's a little math problem
Of logic I designed
Let's see if you get it
Maybe it'll change your mind

If we looked at our population
On any given stance
Their opinion being yay or nay
Has 50 percent chance

And of that 50 percent, there maybe just a quarter Who
actually express that negative thought within their home or
shelter

And of that there are fewer who may respond with violence.
Portrayed by the media
As we search for hope and guidance

15

not sure if this is common sense But
it's adopted by our nation How
exactly do I see it?
Well it's by my education

Education isn't just for math,
or for just training the mind.
Although it induces headaches, Stress
and panic of the kind,

Education makes us think
Something we don't always want to do But in
thinking we translate ideas, Helping me get
this one to you

Ideas are abstract and chaotic Whipping
round like the wind. The only way they
come into form Is when you catch one
and think

But how does one get an idea? How does one
find that spark? How do authors of wonderful
tales find strength to finish their arcs?

Soul fuels the idea

16

An entity separates the mind.
A heart, spirit, whatever it's called Is the
answer one would find

Education trains the soul as well To
stay tall, to understand
For with the impending confusion A
weak soul could not stand

So back to that frequent question
Appearing with academic strife
Education corrects and sharpens your logic It helps
you live your life

Please don't underestimate
Your math and philosophy class
No matter how abstract the subject
They'll always help you pass

6. VOICES

The times when you hear the scariest sounds where
the thoughts are vivid and not like you. When voices
tell you what to do
and no one can hear them but you.
Worry most when you doubt their motives, and
when you feel controlled.
For that is when you lose your grip, and you may ot make it
home.

7. UNREAD

This poem was not meant to be shared or
performed
This poem wasn't meant to be heard For these
are my deepest darkest truths, Unabashed
unabridged and unchanged

This is a battle I fight everyday
Every second that I have to think
Every time I rise from bed
From the death like darkness behind my eyes And the
nullified state of mind

I don't know who I am anymore
Though I know from whence I came From a
loving family with joy and Christ And protection
that allowed me to thrive

But something broke along the way.
Something dark was introduced
Something perverted my mind and my heart That
allowed rage and hatred to spawn.

That something that broke didn't fix with time The
cracks only began to grow.

Isolation, I thought was a solution
But the cold only let new cracks sow.

My confusion began to drown my reason Instead
of seeking help, I fled
I lied to those who loved me
To those who reached out their hands

I fashioned the words that left my lips into a
mask that hid the truths
The truths I feared would taint those who heard it Like the
way it turned my soul

First I was too selfless
Giving myself away
No will of my own
Crippled down to the bone
Trudging through day by day

But then I was too selfish
Anger guided my path
Invisible ropes bound round my soul
I was made of destructive wrath

I have no balance
I have no peace

I suffer in silence
My pain doesn't cease

I tuck it away
I haven't time to cry

I have to keep moving
Or I'll get trapped by the by

I don't want to fight anymore
I can't stand the way I am
The way I work
The way I move
I only push people away

Tears fall from my eyes
When I'm alone and look in the mirror For it's not a reflected
image that I see But my own pain and anger and hatred
towards me

So maybe that's who I am now
Sweet innocent child

Maybe that sweet innocent child is gone That
respectful student of kind nature
Is buried now. It's done.

My creativity came from strife. My
empathy came from strife. But even
so, I fully know
I am not one to enjoy my life.

The mask is all that heeds the now It's all
that I uphold.

8. A FANTASY

Seek not the grail, but the tomb.

Learn the past of the runes.

Make shifts in the plane, regardless of pain, as the morning takes the dew.

The ancient times may now be gone, but the future may forever be lost,

If the one who seeks the price of release, takes on the priceless cost

Read on adventurers, of times unknown In
worlds of false monsters and dames. Roll out
your wits and flimsy courage!
After all, tis only a game

9. COPING

Coping with loss and pain is a skill that everyone needs to
gain
For when it hits, your habits slip, and your joy leaves by
bits

Communication is a difficult learner, for the way words
leave you has been burned within Anxiety fakes urgency
and makes one a difficult listener

Then there is the skeptical, the doubt of what those say when
heard, regardless of who said it or the many times it's surged

This is the weight of the hurt and the scars, that trauma
brings nearer and nearer to hearts

10. FIXATION

Focus is a fleeting thing
He bounces around in the mind and is easily lost to time
Any distraction leaves him scrambling to desert you in
most cases,
Which is why he can be so sacred

However he has a sister, Fixation.
She is stronger, more resilient.
Bending time to her will, she almost forces the mind to
block out everything.
Every thought is altered to obsess over the target at hand.
Unpredictable. Uncontrolled. Unwavering.

These two are the children of productivity. They do not
always have the same effect on the mind after they pass
through. Recovering from either one is its own challenge,
but it is almost never treated as such

11. CHRISTIANITY

Christianity seems to be so full of loathing I am a
christian and even still, i seem to loathe myselfI loathe
my sin, I loathe my body, and I loathe the world I live
in
Is this why the media portrays the Christian as a spiteful
righteousness?
Loathing people for their sin, instead of the sin itself
To the point where hurting their spirit is the way to find
redemption?
God has a rage, we all know, but he is also specific to the
point of its tow
Sin and the sinner are not one bow, do not attack the
person and their soul
Barraging and hatred turns one away, but to
get rid of sin, empathy must stay

12. CONFUSED TRUTH

Happy days are very strange for those with holes in their souls.

It feels like walking on glass panels where you can't seem to believe an illusion

Always waiting for the worse to befall you, leaving you helpless in the ruse

But we must learn to trust those sunny days, and the laughter and the joy

13. WRITER'S BLOCK

Poetry isn't always fluid

It isn't always symmetry

Sometimes it's painstakingly short and morbid Like

death swooping in on battered wings.

14. FAREWELLS

My messages grow shorter as my time here wanes, and
honestly I have no fear

For life isn't trivial, but it can be diabolical. Lord,
why can't I feel you near?

For instead I feel another in my soul...someone who is much
different than I

One who seeks our own destruction, and to leave this
Earth behind

15. THE MOST ONE WANTS TO SAY

The most one wants to say
can never escape their lips,
but gestures and thoughts could portray do much more
than what words could do in a day

16. HUMAN ARITHMETIC

The division of humanity
At an exponential rate
Is something that we as a people Can't
really take
The sums of all our hated
And parabolic curves
Towards people that are different Sprouts
depression death and more No more
rational decisions Or right- angled
thoughts
Towards the fact that adding it all, We're
humans, that's the score Let the fraction
that can see Decide to Help the
remainder be Something more that we
can feel Something that can help us heal.

17. THE STRANGE VARIABLE

A single fading digit among the algorithm, Kicked away as
a deviant, weirdo, lacking rhythm Until I found a home
here
Where I have no reason to fear
I am a missing piece to the expression I
belong here
No need to guesstimate the stakes
My locus posse it's here
Experience increased my probability to do here Now here
is a bit of a proposition, A Call to those who sit here
"If you were given the ability to bring a reckoning, would
you do it all without fear?"
The reckoning of love and hope and just acts The
reckoning of teaching to care and hope to be cared back
To fill the spots of teachers that we truly lack It's a
solution to the problem that we've faced for years,
So let's not slack

18. SHIFTING

Many days pass where I am not me
Where a shell of loathing and silence passes as my visage
Where friends and family believe I act 'strange'

Time passes with a special type of sluggish tone To make hours and days blur onto another Making every step feel obsolete

19. WHAT IS EASY

I can tell you what is easy, and why its often wrong.
Since what is easy may not hurt you, it'll hurt
someone you love.
Easy seems to have no consequence. Easy
seems simple and short.
Easy has nothing to hide or work for, and painless
efforts win all.
But easy is like a treadmill on low speed Easy is
quicksand
Easy means no progress, and that means
nothing at all

20. THANK YOU

For those who have reached the final page, All I
can offer is my thanks.
Bearing with my poems and rants, and I hope you felt some
rise in ranks
Falling in and out of heart can be nothing short of
maddening, but maybe this book has helped you out, and
that my friend, is gladdening

www.ingramcontent.com/pod-product-compliance
Lightning Source LLC
La Vergne TN
LVHW010847200726
843508LV00012B/2785